The pond might look quiet and still, but take a closer look and you'll see it's a small, busy world.

Animals depend on the pond for many things, like water to drink . . .

raccoon

and plants to eat.

bull moose

Many animals begin life in the pond.

Nymphs grow underwater

to become dragonflies.

Tadpoles grow underwater

to become frogs.

Wrigglers grow underwater

to become mosquitoes.

Many plants grow in the pond, too.

water lilies

Plants provide food and are good places for animals to hide.

red-winged blackbird

Can you see the bird hiding here?

green frog

Can you find the frog?

Some birds build their nests in the plants.

red-winged blackbird

The shore is also important.
Turtles lay their eggs there.

snapping turtle

Many plants and animals of the pond are part of the food chain.

male mosquito

Plants are eaten by insects...

archer fish

which are eaten by fish...

great blue heron

which are eaten by birds.

With so many different animals in and around a pond . . .

green crayfish

snail

barred tiger salamander

ducks

what do you think you'll find
the next time you visit one?